INTRODUCTION

It's easy to attract birds to your yard if you provide for their basic needs including food, water, shelter and a safe place to raise their young.

A Bird-Friendly Backyard

1. **Bird Bath** – Locate in an area safe from predators.
2. **Tube Feeder** – Tends to attract smaller seed-eating birds – chickadees, titmice, finches, nuthatches – and discourages larger species.
3. **Nectar Feeder** – A hummingbird magnet.
4. **Berry Bushes** – An important winter food source. The best kind of cover is shrubs or vines that can also provide food for birds.
5. **Brush Pile** – Provides a source of cover that protects birds from the elements and predators.
6. **Suet Feeder** – A high-calorie food source for wintering birds.
7. **Platform Feeder** – Allows birds of all sizes to come and go from all directions.
8. **Native Wildflowers** – Attracts insects and provides nectar.
9. **Nest Box** – Provides a safe place for birds to raise their young.

Most illustrations show the adult male in breeding coloration. Colors and markings may be duller or absent during different seasons. The measurements denote the average maximum length of species from bill to tail tip. Illustrations are not to scale.

A bracketed letter indicates if the species is found predominantly **east (E)** or **west (W)** of the 100th Meridian.

Made in the USA

Waterford Press produces reference guides that introduce novices to nature, science, travel and languages. Product information is featured on the website:
www.waterfordpress.com

Text and illustrations © 2011, 2020 by Waterford Press Inc. All rights reserved.
Cover image © Shutterstock.
Back cover and inside images © iStock Photo.

To order, call 800-434-2555.
For permissions, or to share comments, e-mail editor@waterfordpress.com.
For information on custom-published products, call 800-434-2555 or e-mail info@waterfordpress.com.

ISBN 978-1-58355-946-8
$7.95 U.S.
50795
9 781583 559468
UPC
8 84682 00792 8
10 9 8 7 6 5 4 3 2 1
200901

BIRD FEEDING BASICS – A Folding Pocket Guide to Feeders, Feeds & Common Backyard Birds

Kavanagh/Leung

A POCKET TUTOR® GUIDE

BIRD FEEDING BASICS

A Folding Pocket Guide to Feeders, Feeds & Common Backyard Birds

T0123934

FEEDERS

HOW TO CHOOSE A FEEDER

The most effective way to attract a variety of species to your yard is to put out a number of feeders with different types of food.

Tube Feeder – Dispenses seeds and can host a number of small birds at the same time. Some have very small ports designed to dispense thistle seeds, a favorite of goldfinches and siskins. They may be made of plastic or squirrel-proof wire mesh.

Hopper Feeder – The most popular type of feeder, it attracts a wide variety of species and holds a large quantity of seeds.

Platform (fly-through) Feeder – Attracts the greatest variety of birds (and mammals). Greatest drawbacks are that seeds develop mold rapidly and can become contaminated with bird droppings.

Nectar Feeder – Attracts hummingbirds, orioles, bluebirds and wrens.

Suet Feeder – Hanging bag or cage feeder should be located well out of the reach of pets.

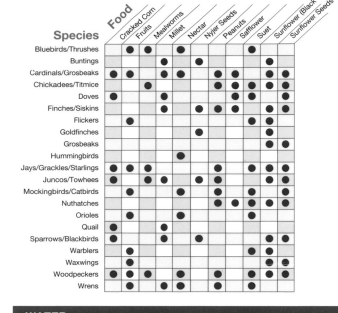

Tube Feeder **Hopper Feeder** **Nectar Feeder** **Platform Feeder** **Suet Feeder**

KEY CONSIDERATIONS WHEN CHOOSING A FEEDER

Will it Keep the Seeds Dry?

Food that becomes exposed to moisture will quickly become contaminated by bacteria like salmonella that can make birds seriously ill. Choose feeders with drainage holes in the bottom of the hoppers and seed tray. Ensure the drainage holes don't become plugged with seeds or shells.

Is it Easy to Clean?

- Feeders should be cleaned regularly to remove bacteria from the hopper, feeding spouts and perches. Dry seed feeders should be cleaned at least once a month or more often when it rains. Nectar feeders should be thoroughly cleaned prior to each refill since the sugary nectar quickly ferments in hot weather.
- The ground beneath outdoor feeders should be cleaned regularly since the fallen seed and husks will become contaminated; they also attract rodents. Rake up and dispose of in the garbage.

Is Capacity Appropriate?

- Hummingbird feeders should hold the amount of nectar the birds can drink in 3-4 days since sugar water ferments quickly in the sun.
- Likewise, dry seed feeders should vary in accordance with the size of the local population. If birds fail to visit a feeder full of seeds, this is your clue that the food is unattractive or the feeder needs to be cleaned thoroughly.

WINDOW ALERT!

An estimated one billion birds die each year by flying into windows. To break up the reflection on windows, cover with screens, hang wind chimes or other obstructions in front of them or attach opaque stickers. To lessen the risk of collisions, keep feeders at least 20 ft. (6 m) away from windows.

FEEDERS

Is it Squirrel-Proof?

Squirrels are incredibly agile, strong, aggressive and clever, and can figure out how to break into almost any feeder. The most common and effective squirrel-proof feeders are:

1. Feeders on a metal pole featuring a guard or baffle (e.g., an inverted metal cone) at the base that squirrels cannot climb over. The pole should be located a minimum of 10 ft. (3 m) from branches, fences, or wires that squirrels can launch themselves from.
2. Tube feeders with a metal mesh (like the one on the cover photo) prevent squirrels from chewing through the side of the feeder. Like all hanging feeders, it should have a squirrel guard or baffle above the wire leading to the feeder.
3. Some feeders have hinged perches that close-up access to food when animals heavier than a bird sit on the perch.

Even nectar isn't safe!

FEEDER FOODS

WHAT TYPE OF FOOD

- **Seeds** – Black-oil sunflower and nyjer seeds are likely the best overall choices for small seed-eaters. Pay careful attention to the content of commercial seed mixtures since many contain bulky fillers – milo, oats, wheat, canola, flax, buckwheat, rice and "mixed grains" – that birds dislike and will waste (birds often sweep their bills from side-to-side to remove these fillers and get at the preferred 'oilers').
- **Suet** (usually beef kidney fat) – High-calorie food source is especially attractive to woodpeckers, chickadees and nuthatches. Regular suet should not be offered at temperatures above 80° F (27° C) since it may melt and turn rancid. A no-melt suet is available that withstands even desert temperatures in summer. A nutritious high-energy substitute for suet is peanut butter.

- **Fruit** – Oranges, bananas and grapes will attract orioles and tanagers (in addition to butterflies!). Raisins attract mockingbirds and blackbirds.
- **Mealworms** (beetle larvae) – Attracts a variety of non seed-cracking birds, including thrushes, wrens, catbirds and warblers.

- **Nectar** – Mix four parts water to one part white sugar. Do not use other sweeteners (e.g. honey) or food coloring; the color of the feeder will attract the birds. Change nectar every other day in summer.

Where to Locate a Feeder?

- Choose a location that has easy access for you in any weather.
- Pick an area where discarded seed husks and bird droppings won't be a clean-up problem.
- Cats kill millions of birds each year. Locate feeders in open areas where birds can see cats approaching or near prickly bushes that cats can't hide in. If you own a cat, attach a bell to its collar to help alert birds of its whereabouts.

FEEDER FOODS

What Species Do You Want to Attract?

The food you set out will determine the type of species you attract.

Species \ Food	Cracked Corn	Fruits	Mealworms	Millet	Nectar	Nyjer Seeds	Peanuts	Safflower	Suet	Sunflower (Black Oil)	Sunflower Seeds
Bluebirds/Thrushes		●	●		●				●		
Buntings				●		●				●	
Cardinals/Grosbeaks	●	●		●	●		●	●		●	●
Chickadees/Titmice			●				●	●	●	●	●
Doves	●			●				●	●		●
Finches/Siskins				●		●	●	●		●	●
Flickers		●							●	●	
Goldfinches						●				●	
Grosbeaks										●	●
Hummingbirds					●						
Jays/Grackles/Starlings	●	●	●				●		●	●	●
Juncos/Towhees	●		●	●		●	●			●	●
Mockingbirds/Catbirds		●			●		●		●		●
Nuthatches							●	●	●	●	●
Orioles		●			●				●		
Quail	●			●							
Sparrows/Blackbirds	●			●		●				●	●
Warblers		●							●	●	
Waxwings		●								●	●
Woodpeckers	●	●	●		●		●		●	●	●
Wrens		●		●	●		●		●		

WATER

Birds require water for drinking and bathing as much or more than they need food. An elevated bird bath is the easiest way to provide them with water and protection from predators.

Bird Baths

Birds bathe to keep their feathers in top shape; dirty feathers inhibit birds' ability to fly and insulate them from the elements. Key features of a good bath are:

- A shallow water reservoir (about 2 in./5 cm deep) that birds can easily dunk into.
- The bath bowl should not be slippery and provide birds with secure footing.
- It should be located where the bird can feel safe and is easy to access.
- Baths that feature trickling or dripping water will attract far more species by sound. The moving water also stops mosquito larvae from developing. Bath accessories like recirculating water pumps, drippers and heaters (for winter) can be purchased from bird supply stores.
- To keep the bath clean, replace the water at least once a week. When greenish algae starts to form on the edges of the bath scrub it off with a dilute 1:10 bleach/water solution.

A NOTE ON NEST BOXES

- Should always be constructed of untreated, unfinished wood at least 1/2 in. (1.3 cm) thick. Cedar and white pine are preferable.
- The lid or floor should be hinged to allow for cleaning.
- Information on the dimensions and placement of species-specific nest boxes are available online or at your local library or bird store.

NATURAL SHELTERS & FOODS

BIRD-FRIENDLY LANDSCAPING

Plant native trees, shrubs and flowers to provide birds with a source of natural food – berries, nuts and seeds – and shelter year-round. Flowers attract insects in spring and fall and provide nectar for hummingbirds. Fruiting shrubs and bushes provide important winter food sources for many species. Your local garden center can provide information on the best native species to plant in your area.

Shelter Plants

Best sources of cover include conifers (pine, spruce, fir, cedar, larch, hemlock, juniper), prickly shrubs (hawthorns, hollies, mesquites, raspberries, blackberries, roses, yews, hickories) and densely leafed broadleaf plants (ashes, cottonwoods, birches, oaks, walnuts, maples, sycamores, willows, dogwoods).

One form of man-made natural habitat you can create for birds are brush piles made from the branches from trees and shrubs and other yard detritus. These piles provide shelter from the elements and safety from predators near feeders and bird baths.

Food Plants

Spring – Shrubs with high sugar content – serviceberries, black cherries, raspberries – are especially attractive to birds during this busy nesting season.

Blackberries turn from red to black in late summer.

Summer – Plants that produce berries May-August will attract species including robins, thrushes, waxwings, orioles, cardinals, thrashers, catbirds, towhees, woodpeckers and grosbeaks. Popular plants include cherry, chokecherry, honeysuckle, raspberry, serviceberry, mulberry, plum, elderberry, blackberry, blueberry, bunchberry and huckleberry.

Oak acorns are a valuable winter food for birds and small mammals.

Autumn – Fall-fruiting plants provide essential nutrients for migratory species and an important food source for wintering species. Plants include spicebush, sassafras, dogwood, mountain ash, winterberry and buffalo-berry. Nut-bearing and acorn-bearing plants including oaks, hickories, walnuts and hazelnuts provide calorie-rich food for jays, woodpeckers and titmice. These plants also offer a prime nesting habitat.

Winter – Winter-fruiting plants have fruit that remains on the plant in winter and are thus readily accessible to wildlife. Fruits that remain on the plant through winter include mountain ash, hawthorns, crabapples, hollies and hackberries.

Clusters of mountain ash berries are an important winter food source.

Landscaping Tips

- A native wildflower mix will attract insects for birds to feed on throughout spring and summer and are also a source of seeds. Tubular flowers like butterflyweed, sage and honeysuckles attract both hummingbirds and butterflies to your garden.
- Stop mowing the back edge of your lawn to give native wildflowers a chance to grow there.
- Rake leaves and grass under your shrubs; as they decompose they'll provide nutrients for your plants and attract insects which, in turn, will attract ground-feeding birds like juncos, towhees, thrashers and thrushes.

Native wildflowers are hardy and attract a wide variety of insects.

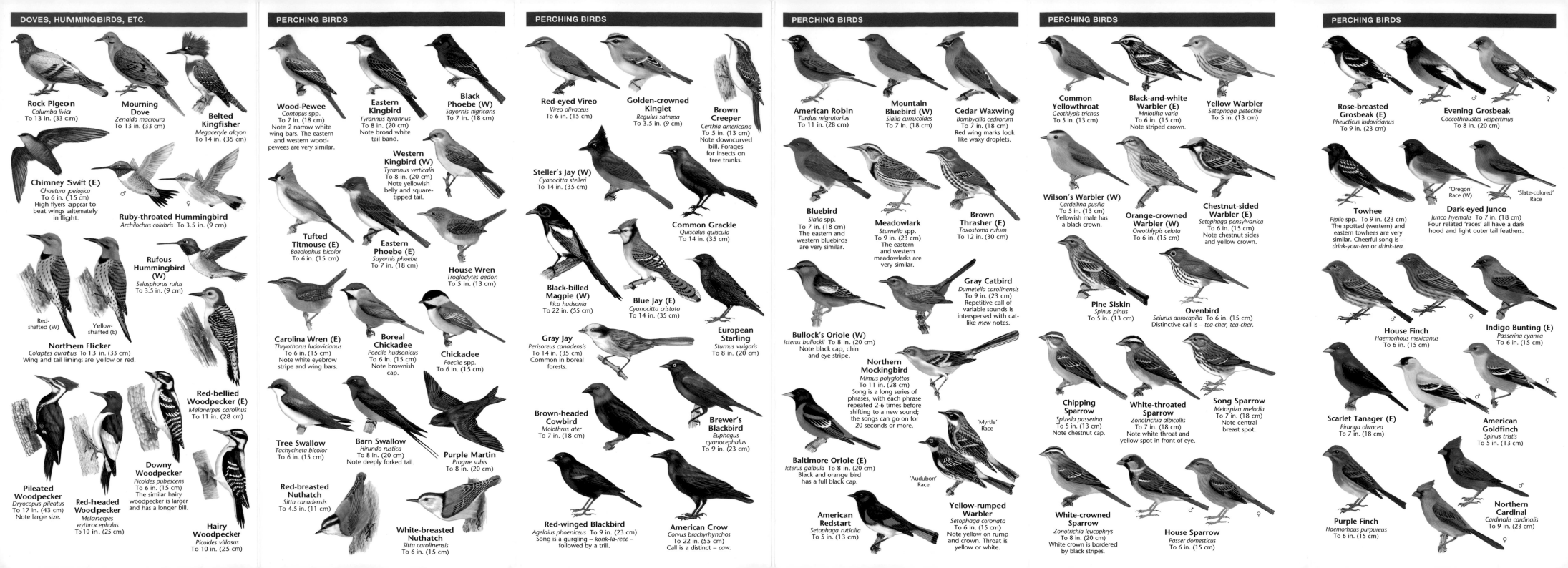

DOVES, HUMMINGBIRDS, ETC.

Rock Pigeon
Columba livia
To 13 in. (33 cm)

Mourning Dove
Zenaida macroura
To 13 in. (33 cm)

Belted Kingfisher
Megaceryle alcyon
To 14 in. (35 cm)

Chimney Swift (E)
Chaetura pelagica
To 6 in. (15 cm)
High flyers appear to beat wings alternately in flight.

Ruby-throated Hummingbird
Archilochus colubris To 3.5 in. (9 cm)

Rufous Hummingbird (W)
Selasphorus rufus
To 3.5 in. (9 cm)

Red-shafted (W)
Yellow-shafted (E)

Northern Flicker
Colaptes auratus To 13 in. (33 cm)
Wing and tail linings are yellow or red.

Red-bellied Woodpecker (E)
Melanerpes carolinus
To 11 in. (28 cm)

Pileated Woodpecker
Dryocopus pileatus
To 17 in. (43 cm)
Note large size.

Red-headed Woodpecker
Melanerpes erythrocephalus
To 10 in. (25 cm)

Downy Woodpecker
Picoides pubescens
To 6 in. (15 cm)
The similar hairy woodpecker is larger and has a longer bill.

Hairy Woodpecker
Picoides villosus
To 10 in. (25 cm)

PERCHING BIRDS

Wood-Pewee
Contopus spp.
To 7 in. (18 cm)
Note 2 narrow white wing bars. The eastern and western wood-pewees are very similar.

Eastern Kingbird
Tyrannus tyrannus
To 8 in. (20 cm)
Note broad white tail band.

Black Phoebe (W)
Sayornis nigricans
To 7 in. (18 cm)

Western Kingbird (W)
Tyrannus verticalis
To 8 in. (20 cm)
Note yellowish belly and square-tipped tail.

Tufted Titmouse (E)
Baeolophus bicolor
To 6 in. (15 cm)

Eastern Phoebe (E)
Sayornis phoebe
To 7 in. (18 cm)

House Wren
Troglodytes aedon
To 5 in. (13 cm)

Carolina Wren (E)
Thryothorus ludovicianus
To 6 in. (15 cm)
Note white eyebrow stripe and wing bars.

Boreal Chickadee
Poecile hudsonicus
To 6 in. (15 cm)
Note brownish cap.

Chickadee
Poecile spp.
To 6 in. (15 cm)

Tree Swallow
Tachycineta bicolor
To 6 in. (15 cm)

Barn Swallow
Hirundo rustica
To 8 in. (20 cm)
Note deeply forked tail.

Purple Martin
Progne subis
To 8 in. (20 cm)

Red-breasted Nuthatch
Sitta canadensis
To 4.5 in. (11 cm)

White-breasted Nuthatch
Sitta carolinensis
To 6 in. (15 cm)

PERCHING BIRDS

Red-eyed Vireo
Vireo olivaceus
To 6 in. (15 cm)

Golden-crowned Kinglet
Regulus satrapa
To 3.5 in. (9 cm)

Brown Creeper
Certhia americana
To 5 in. (13 cm)
Note downcurved bill. Forages for insects on tree trunks.

Steller's Jay (W)
Cyanocitta stelleri
To 14 in. (35 cm)

Common Grackle
Quiscalus quiscula
To 14 in. (35 cm)

Black-billed Magpie (W)
Pica hudsonia
To 22 in. (55 cm)

Blue Jay (E)
Cyanocitta cristata
To 14 in. (35 cm)

European Starling
Sturnus vulgaris
To 8 in. (20 cm)

Gray Jay
Perisoreus canadensis
To 14 in. (35 cm)
Common in boreal forests.

Brown-headed Cowbird
Molothrus ater
To 7 in. (18 cm)

Brewer's Blackbird
Euphagus cyanocephalus
To 9 in. (23 cm)

Red-winged Blackbird
Agelaius phoeniceus To 9 in. (23 cm)
Song is a gurgling – konk-la-reee – followed by a trill.

American Crow
Corvus brachyrhynchos
To 22 in. (55 cm)
Call is a distinct – caw.

PERCHING BIRDS

American Robin
Turdus migratorius
To 11 in. (28 cm)

Mountain Bluebird (W)
Sialia currucoides
To 7 in. (18 cm)

Cedar Waxwing
Bombycilla cedrorum
To 7 in. (18 cm)
Red wing marks look like waxy droplets.

Bluebird
Sialia spp.
To 7 in. (18 cm)
The eastern and western bluebirds are very similar.

Meadowlark
Sturnella spp.
To 9 in. (23 cm)
The eastern and western meadowlarks are very similar.

Brown Thrasher (E)
Toxostoma rufum
To 12 in. (30 cm)

Gray Catbird
Dumetella carolinensis
To 9 in. (23 cm)
Repetitive call of variable sounds is interspersed with cat-like *mew* notes.

Bullock's Oriole (W)
Icterus bullockii To 8 in. (20 cm)
Note black cap, chin and eye stripe.

Northern Mockingbird
Mimus polyglottos
To 11 in. (28 cm)
Song is a long series of phrases, with each phrase repeated 2-6 times before shifting to a new sound; the songs can go on for 20 seconds or more.

'Myrtle' Race

Baltimore Oriole (E)
Icterus galbula To 8 in. (20 cm)
Black and orange bird has a full black cap.

'Audubon' Race

American Redstart
Setophaga ruticilla
To 5 in. (13 cm)

Yellow-rumped Warbler
Setophaga coronata
To 6 in. (15 cm)
Note yellow on rump and crown. Throat is yellow or white.

PERCHING BIRDS

Common Yellowthroat
Geothlypis trichas
To 5 in. (13 cm)

Black-and-white Warbler (W)
Mniotilta varia
To 6 in. (15 cm)
Note striped crown.

Yellow Warbler
Setophaga petechia
To 5 in. (13 cm)

Wilson's Warbler (W)
Cardellina pusilla
To 5 in. (13 cm)
Yellowish male has a black crown.

Orange-crowned Warbler (W)
Oreothlypis celata
To 6 in. (15 cm)

Chestnut-sided Warbler (E)
Setophaga pensylvanica
To 6 in. (15 cm)
Note chestnut sides and yellow crown.

Pine Siskin
Spinus pinus
To 5 in. (13 cm)

Ovenbird
Seiurus aurocapilla To 6 in. (15 cm)
Distinctive call is – tea-cher, tea-cher.

Chipping Sparrow
Spizella passerina
To 5 in. (13 cm)
Note chestnut cap.

White-throated Sparrow
Zonotrichia albicollis
To 7 in. (18 cm)
Note white throat and yellow spot in front of eye.

Song Sparrow
Melospiza melodia
To 7 in. (18 cm)
Note central breast spot.

White-crowned Sparrow
Zonotrichia leucophrys
To 8 in. (20 cm)
White crown is bordered by black stripes.

House Sparrow
Passer domesticus
To 6 in. (15 cm)

PERCHING BIRDS

Rose-breasted Grosbeak (E)
Pheucticus ludovicianus
To 9 in. (23 cm)

Evening Grosbeak
Coccothraustes vespertinus
To 8 in. (20 cm)

'Oregon' Race (W)
'Slate-colored' Race

Towhee
Pipilo spp. To 9 in. (23 cm)
The spotted (western) and eastern towhees are very similar. Cheerful song is – drink-your-tea or drink-tea.

Dark-eyed Junco
Junco hyemalis To 7 in. (18 cm)
Four related 'races' all have a dark hood and light outer tail feathers.

House Finch
Haemorhous mexicanus
To 6 in. (15 cm)

Indigo Bunting (E)
Passerina cyanea
To 6 in. (15 cm)

Scarlet Tanager (E)
Piranga olivacea
To 7 in. (18 cm)

American Goldfinch
Spinus tristis
To 5 in. (13 cm)

Purple Finch
Haemorhous purpureus
To 6 in. (15 cm)

Northern Cardinal
Cardinalis cardinalis
To 9 in. (23 cm)